dolly parton

A PHOTOGRAPHIC CELEBRATION

MOSELEY ROAD INC.
1780 Chemin Queens Park
Gatineau, QC, J9J 1V1, Canada
www.moseleyroad.com

President: Sean Moore
Art and Editorial Director: Lisa Purcell

ISBN: 978-1-62669-404-0

Printed in China

26 25 24 23 22   1 2 3 4 5

dolly parton

A PHOTOGRAPHIC CELEBRATION

edited by lisa purcell

MOSELEY ROAD INC.
GATINEAU, QUEBEC, CANADA

Born January 19, 1946, in a one-room cabin
on the banks of the Little Pigeon River
in Pittman Center, Tennessee,
Dolly Rebecca Parton was the fourth
of twelve children
born to Avie Lee Caroline Owens
and Robert Lee Parton Sr.

Music lives in me . . .
I have the gift of rhyme,
and I'm always trying to write and rhyme.
Music is just natural everyday
occurrence with me."

— *Dolly Parton*

"'I'm going to Nashville to be a star.'
Here was a lot of laughter,
and it kind of embarrassed me,
because to me, that was
what I was going to do.
It was only years later that
I realized that that was just
a big dream for a little kid."

— *Dolly, on telling her Tennessee
classmates about future plans*

"In the early days, I think it used to bother me
when people [made fun of me].
It didn't change me. It didn't make me do it different,
but I kind of get a little embarrassed sometimes
if somebody made too much fun of it.
That was when I knew they didn't know
who all I was or what all I was."

— *Dolly Parton*

"If you don't like the road you're walking,
start paving another one."

— *Dolly Parton*

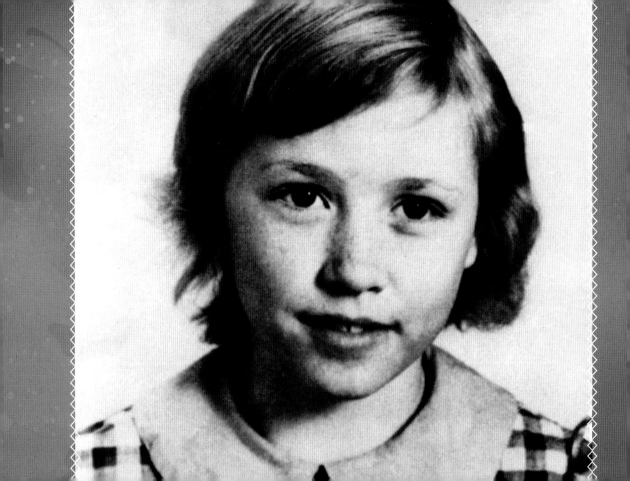

"I was probably seven years old when I started playing the guitar and writing some serious songs."

— *Dolly Parton*

"I learned early on that
I could get a lot of attention
by singing and writing little songs,
so it was like throwing nuts to a monkey. . .
I just couldn't get enough."

— *Dolly Parton*

Dolly's path to stardom began
when as a child
she sang on local radio
and television programs
in the East Tennessee area.
At 13, she recorded the single "Puppy Love"
and appeared at the Grand Ole Opry,
where she first met Johnny Cash,
who encouraged her to follow her instincts
when it came to her career.
Dolly was inducted into the
Grand Ole Opry in 1969.

"I told Dolly, she would be a gigantic movie star someday. And she said, 'I think you have lost your mind'."

— *Fred Foster, owner of the Monument Records, Dolly's first recording label, in 1965*

"They recorded me rock!
I guess they figured my voice
was so weird that the country people
would never go for it."

— *Dolly, on recording her first records*

"The magic is inside you.
There ain't no crystal ball."

— *Dolly Parton*

"People just relate to me.
They know I'm a regular person
brought up in a hardworking, poor family,
that I've had all the struggles that people have."

— *Dolly Parton*

"I know who I am;
I know what I can and can't do.
I know what I will and won't do.
I know what I am capable of,
and I don't agree to do things that
I don't think I can pull off."

— *Dolly Parton*

"It was always my dream
that when I graduated from high school
that I was going to move to Nashville.
My daddy wouldn't have let me go before then anyway.
He'd have sent a posse after me if I had left home.
So I stayed in school, even though I didn't like it."

— *Dolly Parton*

"I had my songs to sing,
I had an ambition,
and it burned inside me.
It was something I knew
would take me out of the mountains.
I knew I could see worlds
beyond the Smoky Mountains."

— *Dolly Parton*

"I didn't know what was awaiting me.
I didn't know what I was going to do.
But I knew I didn't have to worry about being poor,
because I couldn't have been any poorer
than we were there at home."

— *Dolly, on moving to Nashville*

Dolly credits her mother as the source
of her own musical abilities.
Avie Lee, despite her poor health,
still managed to keep house and entertain her children
with Smoky Mountain folklore and ancient ballads.

"If you talk bad about country music,
it's like saying bad things about my momma.
Them's fightin' words."

— *Dolly Parton*

"Womanhood was a difficult thing
to get a grip on in those hills,
unless you were a man."

— *Dolly, on her rural Tennessee upbringing*

"I didn't want to get married.
All I had ever known was housework
and kids and workin' in the fields.
But I didn't want to be domestic,
I wanted to be free."

— *Dolly Parton*

On May 30, 1966,
Dolly married Carl Thomas Dean
in Ringgold, Georgia.
Dean has always avoided the limelight,
keeping a low profile throughout his wife's career.

"We're completely opposite,
but that's what makes it fun.
I never know what he's gonna say or do.
He's always surprising me."

— *Dolly, on her marriage to Carl Dean*

"Not everyone is lucky enough to be
with someone for 50 years,
but I have been.
He has been the love of my life
and the life of my love."

— *Dolly, on her marriage to Carl Dean*

In 1967, musician and country music entertainer Porter Wagoner offered Dolly a regular spot on his weekly syndicated television program *The Porter Wagoner Show*. By the next year, the Country Music Association named the duo Vocal Group of the Year.

"Porter and I fought like cats and dog. My husband and I have never fought, and Porter and I did nothing but fight."

— Dolly, on her relationship with musical partner Porter Wagoner

"I often get myself in love trouble
because I'm so passionate;
I love so much and so deep."

— *Dolly Parton*

"He had a bad temper, and when it flared, it flared, but when he was in good spirits, he was a joy."

— *Dolly, on Porter Wagoner*

"You do have a relationship. And it is based in passion.
You have to experience emotions if you're going to sing a song
like 'Lost Forever in Your Kiss.' You're living with these people,
day in and day out. Whether it's a love affair or not, you're all in,
in the relationship. Whether it's sexual or whether it's just passionate,
you are connected. It's a love-hate relationship.
It is a marriage, of a sort."

— *Dolly, on her relationship with musical partner Porter Wagoner*

"Storms make trees take deeper roots."

— *Dolly Parton*

"He was trying to control something that's not controllable, and that was making him miserable and me miserable."

— *Dolly, on working with Porter Wagoner*

"Sometimes it was easy, sometimes not.
We were both very bullheaded."

— *Dolly, on her relationship with musical partner Porter Wagoner*

Porter
and Dolly

THE ESSENTIAL PORTER WAGONER AND DOLLY PARTON

THE ESSENTIAL PORTER WAGONER AND DOLLY PARTON

"I wrote that song to say,
'Here's how I feel.
I will always love you,
but I have to go.'"

*— Dolly, on the inspiration behind "I Will Always Love You,"
which she wrote and first recorded in 1973*

~~~~~

"That's the best song you ever wrote.
And you can go, if I can produce that song."

— Porter Wagoner, on his reaction to "I Will Always Love You"

"We cannot direct the wind,
but we can adjust the sails."

— *Dolly Parton*

"My weaknesses
have always been
food and men
— in that order."

— *Dolly Parton*

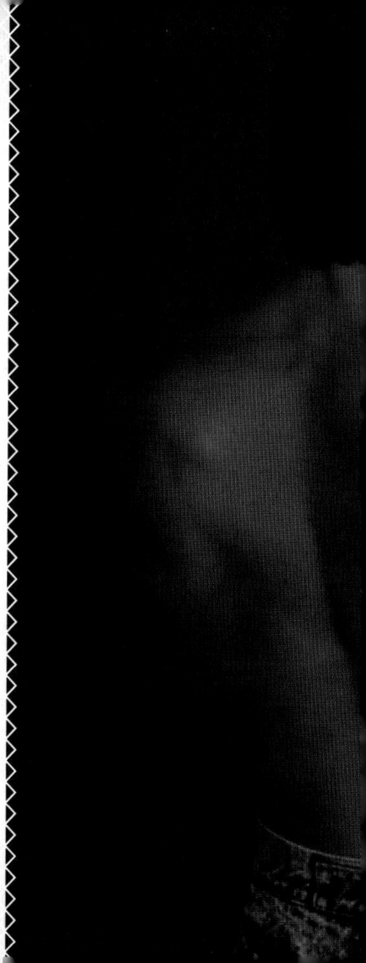

"I've . . . been accused
of being involved
with every man I'm ever
seen with or worked with.
Maybe I have, maybe I ain't.
I never tell if I have."

– *Dolly Parton*

Her first full-length album,
Hello, I'm Dolly, came out in 1967
and spawned two Top 40 hits,
"Dumb Blonde" and "Something Fishy."

"I'm not offended by all
the dumb blonde jokes
because I know I'm not dumb—
and I'm not blonde either."

— *Dolly Parton*

"The songs lead to everything else.
Everything that I am starts with that song.
No matter who you are as an artist,
if you don't have a great song,
you're not going anywhere."

— *Dolly Parton*

"I make jokes about it, but it's the truth
that I kind of patterned my look after the town tramp.
I didn't know what she was, just this woman who was blond
and piled her hair up, wore high heels and tight skirts,
and, boy, she was the prettiest thing I'd ever seen.
Momma used to say, 'Aw, she's just trash,'
and I thought, that's what I want to be
when I grow up. Trash."

— *Dolly Parton*

"It costs a lot of money
to look this cheap."

— *Dolly Parton*

"I often wonder what my calling
really was because I often thought
I was born for a purpose
other than just to be a country singer."

— *Dolly Parton*

"You'll never do a whole lot
unless you're brave enough to try."

— *Dolly Parton*

"I don't listen to music for fun.
I ain't got enough time for fun!
I'm always busy writing my own music.
I don't try to compete or
see what other people are doing."

— *Dolly Parton*

In February 1971, Dolly released "Joshua,"
her first solo number 1 single.
In October 1973, she released "Jolene,"
her second solo number 1 single on the country charts.
It reached the top position in February 1974.
"Jolene" was ranked No. 217
on *Rolling Stone* magazine's list of the
"500 Greatest Songs of All Time" in 2004.

"Sometimes a song just has to cater
to whatever's goin' on.
A well-written song
is a song that stays
true to the subject."

— *Dolly Parton*

"It's about a girl
who was trying to steal my husband
when we first met.
I put a stop to that, obviously."

— *Dolly, on the story behind "Jolene"*

Dolly says "Jolene" is the song
most recorded by other artists
of all the songs she has written.

"Oh, I used to write a lot
of sad-ass songs."

— *Dolly Parton*

"A lot of my heartbreak songs
are inspired by things my sisters
are going through, or friends."

— *Dolly Parton*

"Well, my family's very musical,
and everybody played
musical instruments,
so we just grabbed up anything
and tried to play."

— *Dolly Parton*

In 2916, Dolly appeared with Randy Parton
and the Parton Family Band in
Hallmark Channel's *Home and Family*.
Her brother Randy, who passed away from cancer
in 2021 at the age of 67 in Pigeon Forge, Tennessee,
was a singer-songwriter, actor, and businessman.

Dolly's younger sister Stella
followed in the steps of her big sister,
launching a successful career
as a singer, songwriter, and actor.

"I'm not going to limit myself
just because people won't accept
the fact that I can do something else."

— *Dolly Parton*

"I can write a song
in about an hour
if it's a simple country song."

— *Dolly Parton*

"I said, 'I'm really sorry,'
and I cried all night. I mean,
it was like the worst thing.
You know, it's like, Oh, my God . . . Elvis Presley.'
And other people were saying,
'You're nuts. It's Elvis Presley.' . . .
I said, 'I can't do that.
Something in my heart says, 'Don't do that.
And I just didn't do it. . . . He would have killed it.
But anyway, so he didn't.
Then when Whitney came out,
I made enough money to buy Graceland."

— Dolly, on being unable to let Elvis Presley record "I Will Always Love You"

"I was on my way home, and I turned the radio on,
and all of a sudden I heard that acapella part,
and I was like 'Wooo! What's that?'
By the time it dawned on me what I was hearing
when she went into that chorus
I had to stop the car because I almost wrecked.
I thought my heart was going to just bust right out of my body.
It was the most powerful feeling that I've ever had
'cause it was such a shock,
and it was so great, and she sang it so good
that I was just overwhelmed."

— Dolly on the first time she heard
Whitney Houston's recording of "I Will Always Love You"

"The way I see it,
if you want the rainbow,
you gotta put up with the rain."

— *Dolly Parton*

"We can't all be stars; we can't all be leaders.
We are all God's creatures, living life, and we have that God light
in us and we're supposed to let it shine. And not everybody wants
to be like me and stick their neck out to get up on stage and perform.
There are those like me, but there are also those that are of a shyer nature.
And they're smarter than most of us that are out there showing our asses."

— *Dolly Parton*

"No one picks like a Nashville picker picks,
but no one makes me grin
quite like you, Carol Burnett!"

— Dolly, via Twitter

Veteran entertainer Bob Hope was one of the guests on the second incarnation of her TV show *Dolly* in 1988. She had also appeared on *Bob Hope's Jolly Christmas* special that same year.

"I've had offers lots of times
to do some acting,
but I don't care to act."

— Dolly, on acting in a 1967 interview

"I have never done any acting at all,
never thought I'd be particularly good at it.
But the people at 20th Century-Fox
really feel like I can be, or that I am, a natural actress."

— *Dolly, in a 1978* Playboy *magazine interview*

Dolly landed a leading role
portraying secretary Doralee in
the 1980 comedy 9 *to* 5,
which highlights discrimination
against women in the workplace
and co-starred Jane Fonda and Lily Tomlin.

"They were seeking me,
which made me feel even prouder.
This was not the first movie I was offered;
it was the first one I accepted."

— *Dolly, about taking up her role in* 9 to 5

Dolly

9 to 5 and
Odd Jobs

Dolly became one of the few female country singers
to simultaneously have a number 1 single
on the country and pop charts,
when "9 to 5" hit number 1 on both.
This theme song from the 1980 movie of the
same name also received an Academy Award
nomination for Best Original Song.

"Jane Fonda and I were just flabbergasted.
We thought it was so great.
I said to Jane, this will make the movie
a hit if nothing else."

*— Lily Tomlin, on Fonda's and her reaction
to hearing the song "9 to 5" for the first time*

"A lot of people were sayin',
'Boy, I would l-o-o-o-v-e to see that.
There ain't no way them three b******
are gonna get along!
Can you imagine three women like that?!'
And you know, we had the greatest time."

— *Dolly, on working with Jane Fonda and Lily Tomlin in 9 to 5*

"*Nine to Five* fascinated me,
and I knew instantly that I should do it —
I knew that it was a career move.
And it fell together really well —
just according to my lists."

— *Dolly, about taking up her role in* 9 to 5

'Don't worry about acting.
Just be yourself.
The director will tell you what to do,
and you'll learn."

— *Jane Fonda, advising Dolly on acting*

"Dabney Coleman
[who played Mr. Hart]
taught me a lot, too.
He's a Texas guy,
and we had a great connection.
They all knew it was my first time
in the movies, so they were all helpful.
People are generous."

— *Dolly, on her experience filming 9 to 5*

"Dolly is a person of heart and spirit.
She's not a political person,
but we need more like her.
She is profound,
and she has a really, really huge heart,
and she's really smart and deeply spiritual."

— *Jane Fonda, on Dolly*

"I don't really like getting up on TV
and saying political things.
I don't even want to make a deal out of it,
but I want people to know I'm my own individual self."

— *Dolly Parton*

"I don't think . . . I mean, I must be
if being a *feminist* means I'm all for women, yes.
But I don't feel I have to march,
hold up a sign or label myself.
I think the way I have conducted my life
and my business and myself speaks for itself.
I don't think of it as being feminist.
It's not a label I have to put on myself.
I'm just all for gals."

— *Dolly Parton*

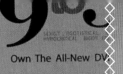

Dolly wrote the score for
9 to 5: The Musical,
a musical-theater adaptation
of the feature film *9 to 5*
that opened in 2008.
She received nominations
for a Drama Desk Award
for Outstanding Music
and a Drama Desk Award
for Outstanding Lyrics,
as well as a Tony Award nomination
for Best Original Score.

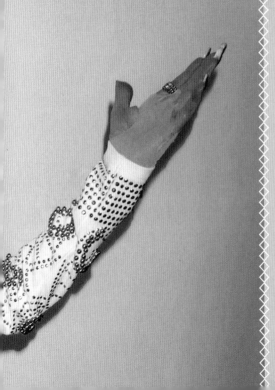

"I don't know what
goin' Hollywood means;
if it means goin' to sh*t."

— *Dolly Parton*

"It's important to me that
I accomplish things as a human being,
as it should be to all people to accomplish
all that they can without sacrificing other people.
I didn't sacrifice the happiness
of other people to get where I am."

— *Dolly Parton*

"I feel glamorous on the inside,
so I want to look like it on the outside."

— *Dolly Parton*

"In my head, I knew where I was headed
because to me, I'm not a natural beauty.
I wanted to be pretty.
I was that backwoods Barbie;
I was impressed with that
and, I just always felt more inside
than how I looked on the outside."

— *Dolly Parton*

"I always loved the *Frederick's of Hollywood* magazines. That was just kind of to me how I felt, like I wanted to look."

— *Dolly Parton*

"I would never stoop so low
as to be fashionable."

— *Dolly Parton*

"I always imagined
Dolly's apartment's closet opens,
and sequins come flying out!"

— *Actor Reese Witherspoon, who got to raid Dolly's closet*

"People always ask me how long
it takes to do my hair.
I don't know, I'm never there."

— *Dolly Parton*

"All I am saying is every year
I've been on the CMA awards show,
even when I was just presenting,
they have always asked me to wear less hair and make-up.
Then I would be like everybody else,
and I don't want to be like everybody else.
I'm not doing anything to be different.
I just don't follow people's trends.
I've got to do what I want to do and wear
my makeup and hair like I want to."

— *Dolly, on being asked to reduce her famous "big" hair
or lighten her trademark makeup*

"I may look fake
but I'm real where it counts."

— *Dolly Parton*

"People know that I wear a lot of hair.
They already know I wear makeup.
My country music fans have already accepted that fact.
It's the people who don't know no different
that are trying to change me all the time.
But they aren't gonna change me."

— *Dolly Parton*

"I'm little. I'm only five feet tall.
I've always had a complex
about being short,
so I like my hair high."

— *Dolly Parton*

"You never know if you're going to wreck the bus,
you never know if you're going to be
somewhere in a hotel and there's going to be a fire.
So I leave my makeup on at night
and clean my face in the morning."

— *Dolly Parton*

"I have pretty good skin
considering my age,
and I think a lot of it is
mineral oil and bacon grease."

— *Dolly, on her beauty regimen*

"I don't keep up with a lot of trends.
I've never been a fashion horse.
I'm so busy writing my songs,
trying to maintain my business,
and all the new things that come along.
I stay working all the time."

— *Dolly Parton*

"I have had clothes bust apart
on stage, seriously I have. . . .
I wear my clothes awfully tight."

— *Dolly Parton*

"I don't know that I'm beautiful or glamorous.
I'm a pretty artificial looking person.
I sure am flattered when people think I'm beautiful,
but I think I'm leaning towards
more cartoonish than beautiful."

— *Dolly Parton*

"I ain't gonna never change
unless I want to.
I don't try to follow no styles.
I told you this before, and I'll tell anybody else.
I ain't in style, but I like to think I've got my own style."

— *Dolly Parton*

"I have to stay on a low-carb diet
when I'm on the road
because my show clothes are so tight . . .
There is nothing more uncomfortable
than trying to wear those tight-ass clothes
when you're too big for them!"

— *Dolly Parton*

"I'm comfortable with who I am.
And since I wasn't born as a natural beauty,
I just make the most of what I've got."

— *Dolly Parton*

"If I see something saggin',
baggin', or draggin',
I'm gone have it nipped,
tucked, or sucked!"

— *Dolly Parton*

The association of breasts
with Parton's public image is illustrated
in the naming of Dolly the sheep after her,
because the sheep was cloned
from a cell taken from an
adult ewe's mammary gland.

"I was the first woman to burn my bra—
it took the fire department four days to put it out."

— *Dolly Parton*

"I've always been pretty well blessed.
People are always asking if they're real. . . .
I tell you what. These are mine."

— *Dolly, on her famously ample bosom*

"I have certain guidelines on the show.
But I would give about a year's pay
to peek under there."

— Classic talk show host Johnny Carson,
when discussing Dolly's attributes on The Tonight Show

"'Big T' stood for 'Big Texas'.
So that's what I wanted to call the movie.
Someone said, 'You can't call it that.'
I said,' Why not?'
They said, 'Because everybody's going
to think it stands for your big T's.
I said, 'That goes to show you how
everybody's mind goes to that place.'
Any titty joke, they'll go for."

— *Dolly, on changing the name of the TV movie she wrote,
along with Mark Kiracofe, to* Wild Texas Wind

Although Dolly turned down several offers to pose nude for *Playboy* magazine, she did appear on the cover of the October 1978 issue wearing the iconic Playboy bunny outfit.

"In the mountains in the South,
the traditional and only ways
for a woman to escape poverty
were either to marry
or to run off and become
something like a stripper. . . .
Okay, I thought about bein' a stripper,
but I decided that I really better not."

— *Dolly Parton*

"It's a good thing I was born a girl,
otherwise I'd be a drag queen."

— *Dolly Parton*

@GUSCUNT

"I am not gay, but if I were
I would be the first one
running out of the closet."

— *Dolly Parton*

"I always had a very open mind
and a very open heart.
I always look for the good in everybody
and the God in everybody.
I play to that. And I just love people.
I love the difference in people.
I love getting to know people.
I appreciate getting accepted myself,
because I know I'm unusual.
And I love the unusual in other people."

— *Dolly Parton*

"I think we've just become so divided,
'cause people just seem to love to hate."

— *Dolly Parton*

"I'm just a friendly person.
And I hopefully have a good sense of humor.
People get a kick out of my stupidity."

— *Dolly Parton*

"We're not all perfect.
People always say to me:
"Oh you seem happy all the time."
But I'm not happy all the time.
I'm a human being. I'm very sensitive.
I hurt like anybody else.
But I do try my best to have a good attitude
and I set about tryin' to take care of myself
knowing I'm not going to be exactly right,
so I just try to see what I can do
to improve every single day."

— *Dolly Parton*

"I don't make people bend over backwards,
and I don't like that in people.
I am definitely no diva."

— *Dolly Parton*

"Dolly Parton spent about half an hour
shaking everybody's hand
and leaving behind a wake
of people telling each other,
'Gee, she's really nice,'
as if, well, as if somehow
she shouldn't have been."

— *Film critic Roger Ebert, on Dolly*

"Even people
who hate everyone
love Dolly Parton."

— *Fran Lebowitz*

"They think I'm simpleminded
because I seem to be happy.
Why shouldn't I be happy?
I have everything I ever wanted and more.
Maybe I am simpleminded.
Maybe that's the key: simple."

— *Dolly Parton*

"The magic with me is
that I look completely false
when I'm completely real."

— *Dolly Parton*

"A great smile is a wonderful asset,
but a good heart is pure gold."

— *Dolly Parton*

"I just want you to know
I'm proud of you.
I think you're great.
I hope you'll be around
for 100 more years to hang
out with me, if nothing else."

— *Dolly, on Cher*

"When someone shows you
their true colors, believe them."

— *Dolly Parton*

"Smile — it increases your face value."

— *Dolly Parton*

"Sometimes my mouth is a little too big
and a little too open and
sounds too much like a sailor."

— *Dolly Parton*

"Wouldn't it be something
if we could have things we love in abundance
without their losing that special attraction
the want of them held for us."

— *Dolly Parton*

"If I had to choose just one thing to be,
I would choose to be a songwriter."

— *Dolly Parton*

In 2019, *Dolly Parton's Heartstrings*
premiered on Netflix.
The anthology series examines
"the stories, memories and inspirations
behind Parton's most beloved songs."
Her signature "Jolene"
was the first song showcased.

Dolly can't read sheet music,
but she can play quite a few instruments,
including the dulcimer, autoharp,
banjo, guitar, electric guitar, fiddle,
piano, recorder, and the saxophone.

"I play some of everything.
I ain't that good at none of it,
but I try to sell it.
I really try to lay into it."

— *Dolly Parton*

"If I had to give up performing,
it wouldn't bother me too much.
But I couldn't live without my writing.
I put all my feelings,
my very soul, into my writing.
I tell the world in my songs things
I wouldn't even tell my husband."

— *Dolly Parton*

"I just love the wee hours.
I'm just an early bird.
I get more work done
between three and seven
than most people all day,
because it's quiet
and the energy's all low-key,
except mine."

— *Dolly Parton*

"Some of my very best songs
I've written within
30 minutes' time."

— *Dolly Parton*

"A lot of people write about their own experiences.
I wrote some about my own experiences,
but not really that much because I write a lot of sad songs
and I just write about things I've seen happen
or things that have been in the family or things I've read.
And in a general conversation with somebody,
I might just get some good ideas.
I just write. I don't know where I get my ideas.
I don't really go out to look for any,
they just seem to come natural."

— *Dolly, on where she gets her song ideas*

"I write a lot of songs about women
because I am a woman,
or I just write songs that women experience.
But I write a lot of songs for men.
In fact, I've had hit songs,
you know, about men.
I write — you know,
I write songs about my dad.

— *Dolly Parton*

"If there's something you know
and there's something you feel,
but you can't quite express it,
you will hear it somewhere.
And you don't have to worry,
because someone will
get it sung out."

— *Dolly Parton*

"I'm so thankful I can write songs.
I can capture all those
memories in my songs
and keep those memories alive."

— *Dolly Parton*

"Sometimes I'll be writin' a song
and I'll be cookin' or I'll be doin' this or that
and I'll just be thinkin' while I'm doin' it
and I just write when I think of a good line.
I just think before I write it down."

— *Dolly, on her song-writing process*

"Sometimes—I think most everybody does this—
I dream of songs. I dream of writin' songs.
Sometimes I can remember 'em the next mornin'
and then sometimes I can't.
Usually I get a lot of good ideas in the night.
I guess it's 'cause it's so quiet.
I'll get up and write 'em down
and maybe finish them the next morning.
And then maybe I'll just stay up and write 'em.
It depends on how knocked-out I am!
So my ideas just come from different places.
I get inspired from different things."

— *Dolly, on her song-writing process*

"God is in everything I do
and all my work
glorifies Him."

– *Dolly Parton*

"My songs are the door to every dream
I've ever had and every success I've ever achieved."

— *Dolly Parton*

"You are the song of every bird,
you are the poet's every word,
every artist's picture,
every writer's play."

— *Dolly Parton*

"I write songs for men and about men
and their feelings too,
because I know how they feel.
I look like a woman,
but I think like a man.
But I think like a woman, too."

— *Dolly Parton*

"My nails are my rhythm section
when I'm writing a song all alone.
Someday, I may cut an album,
just me and my nails."

— *Dolly Parton*

"I was always such a feisty little thing
and I was always doing stuff backstage or onstage.
You know, pinch him on the butt or whatever."

— *Dolly, on teasing Kenny Rogers*

"We had a real chemistry
and love people talking about it.
It was great to hear people talking about it
and (she'd wink) and I would wink back.
But we were too good of friends."

— *Kenny Rogers, about rumors that
he and Dolly were more than just friends*

"He's been married about 40 times!
Couldn't catch him between wives!"

— *Dolly, joking about her interest in Kenny Rogers*

Dolly's second film role was as
Miss Mona Stangley in 1982's
The Best Little Whorehouse in Texas,
co-starring Burt Reynolds.

"I couldn't wait to
jump into bed with Burt Reynolds.
In the movie, not in real life."

— *Dolly, on working with Burt Reynolds
in* The Best Little Whorehouse in Texas

"Wouldn't you feel like you wasted five dollars
if you paid to see *Whorehouse*
and you didn't see me and Burt kiss?
I was makin' a joke, and I stuck to it —
I'm not going to miss my chance to kiss Burt Reynolds."

*— Dolly, on working with Burt Reynolds
in* The Best Little Whorehouse in Texas

"I got to work with her for so long
that eventually I was looking at her face."

— *Burt Reynolds, on Dolly*

"I know we will always remember his funny laugh,
that mischievous sparkle in his eyes,
and his quirky sense of humor.
You will always be my favorite sheriff,
rest in peace my little buddy,
and I will always love you, Dolly."

— *Dolly, on the passing of Burt Reynolds*

"I tried every diet in the book.
I tried some that weren't in the book.
I tried eating the book.
It tasted better than most of the diets."

— *Dolly Parton*

"Well, I can't eat.
I can't just sit here
and feel sorry for myself.
Why don't I just write a song?"

*— Dolly, on distracting herself
from the rigors of a weight-loss diet*

"He is into physical fitness
and was shocked at the junk food I ate.
I think that's when I began to realize that
I should change my ways and get healthier."

— *Dolly, on Sylvester Stallone's influence on her eating habits*

"When I met him,
I loved him instantly.
I think we just struck up
a wonderful lasting friendship.
I loved his energy and his personality.
He was very protective of me."

— *Dolly, on Sylvester Stallone*

"He had me laughing,
I couldn't even do my scenes.
They just left my laughing in,
because I was laughing in places
where I wasn't supposed to.
I was supposed to be acting.
He absolutely tickles me to death.
He's a crazy person."

— *Dolly, on working with Sylvester Stallone
in 1984's* Rhinestone

"It's true that Sylvester Stallone
cannot sing country music.
But I'll tell you what he can sing:
old '50s rock 'n' roll songs."

*— Dolly, on working with Sylvester Stallone
in 1984's* Rhinestone

"The most fun I ever had on a movie was with Dolly Parton on *Rhinestone*."

— *Sylvester Stallone, on working with Dolly*

"Even though the movie did not do well
and didn't get good reviews,
if you listen to the songs I wrote for it, they hold up.
I enjoyed writing that as much
as anything I've ever done."

— *Dolly, on writing songs for 1984's* Rhinestone

"It's hard to be a diamond
in a rhinestone world."

— *Dolly Parton*

Dolly received her first star
on the Hollywood Walk of Fame in 1984,
along with *Rhinestone* costar Sylvester Stallone.
In 2018, she was awarded yet another star,
this time in recognitions of her album *Trio*
with Emmylou Harris and Linda Ronstadt.

In 1987 Dolly released *Trio*
with Emmylou Harris
and Linda Ronstadt
to critical acclaim.

Dolly played a beautician alongside
Sally Field, Shirley MacLaine, Daryl Hannah,
Olympia Dukakis, and Julia Roberts
in *Steel Magnolias*, a 1989 comedy-drama film
about the bond a group of women share
in a small-town Louisiana southern community.

"When I was young and had nothing,
I wanted to be rich and famous,
and now I am.
So I'm not going to
complain about anything."

— *Dolly, to co-star Julia Roberts
while filming* Steel Magnolias
*when Roberts wondered
how Dolly could stay so calm*

Dolly partnered with
fellow country superstars
Tammy Wynette
and Loretta Lynn
in 1993 for their
Honky Tonk Angels album.
It went certified gold
about two months
after its release.

"Well, I'm not the queen, though.
The Queen of Country Music is Kitty Wells.
Then there are the others like
Loretta [Lynn] and Tammy [Wynette]."

— *Dolly, rejecting the title of "Queen of Country Music"*

"We prefer the title Patron Saint of Appalachia. Dolly Parton has done so much for the region that the title fits her like a glove."

— *Outside.com, on Dolly's rejection of the title "Queen of Country Music"*

Dolly starred in her first dramatic role
on television in 1992 in an
NBC-TV World Premiere Movie-of-the-Week,
Wild Texas Wind with Gary Busey.

"In the film, Gary Busey was being abusive.
'Gary Abusey' is what I said as a joke.
I thought he did a really good job,
but people didn't like to see me getting beat up.
I think my fans don't want to see me playing that kind of role."

— *Dolly, on fans' reaction to her role as Theola Rayfield in* Wild Texas Wind

In 1998, *Nashville Business* ranked her
the wealthiest country music star.
As of 2017, her net worth
was estimated at $500 million.

"My songs are like my children—
I expect them to support me when I'm old."

— *Dolly Parton*

"Honestly, being put into the Songwriters Hall of Fame,
with all the great people in there,
would have to be one of the greater compliments
that anyone could ever be paid.
I don't know that I'm deserving,
but it makes me want to go out and write songs."

— *Dolly, being honored with the Songwriters Hall of Fame Award
from the National Academy of Popular Music in 2001*

"I love the fans. I love that energy. It just really is restoring.
You know when you're first in love, how it energizes you?
I get that from the fans. That's a great empowering, restoring kind
of energy. I think entertainers are addicted to that feeling.
It's . . . just knowing that you can do something to
change somebody's life or make somebody happy,
even if it's just for an evening."

— *Dolly Parton*

"Leave something good
in every day."

— *Dolly Parton*

Dolly teamed up with Queen Latifah
in the musical film *Joyful Noise*,
playing a choir director's widow
who joins forces with Latifah's character
to save a small Georgia town's gospel choir.

Dolly shares the record
of the most number 1 Billboard
country music charts songs
with country legend Reba McEntire.

Dolly's many honors include:

Recording Industry Association of America–certified gold, platinum, and multi-platinum awards;

25 Billboard country music charts number 1 songs;

44 career Top 10 country albums (a record for any artist);

110 career-charted singles;

11 Grammy Awards and 50 nominations, including the Lifetime Achievement Award;

10 Country Music Association Awards, including Entertainer of the Year (one of only seven female artists to win this award);

5 Academy of Country Music Awards, including Entertainer of the Year;

4 People's Choice Awards; and 3 American Music Awards.

In 1999, Dolly was inducted into the Country Music Hall of Fame.

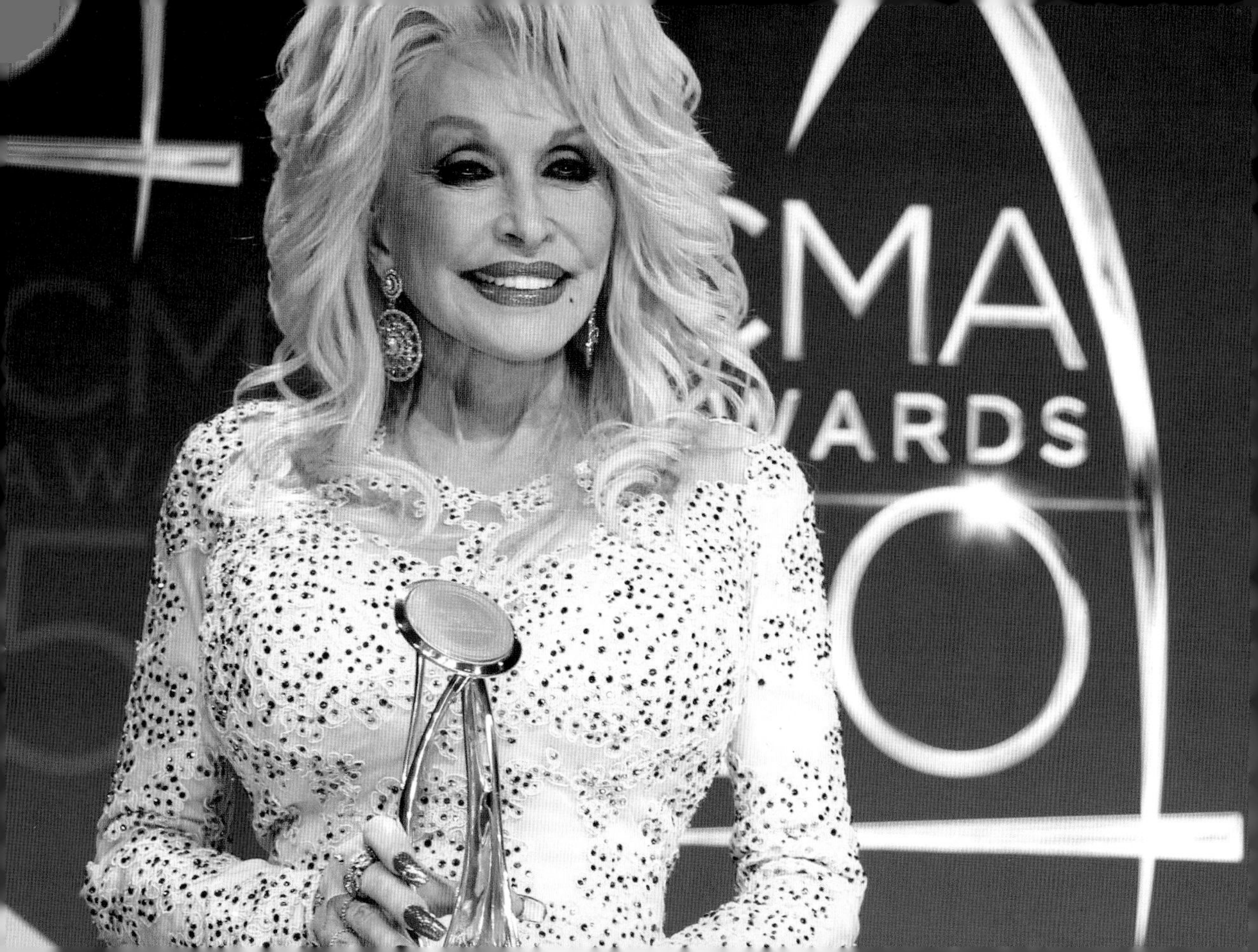

"I think of country radio like a great lover:
you were nice to me,
you gave me a lot of cool stuff,
and then you dumped my ass
for another woman."

— *Dolly Parton*

"You should have sent me a sack of dope."

— *Dolly, on her difficulty singing with Willie Nelson*

A bronze sculpture of Dolly,
which the citizens of her hometown erected
on the courthouse lawn in Sevierville, Tennessee,
is one her most cherished honors.
The statue portrays her as a young woman,
barefoot and perched on a rock
while casually strumming her guitar.

355

Dolly appears with other country artists, including Johnny Cash, Keith Urban, Reba McEntire, Loretta Lynn, Garth Brooks, Blake Shelton, and Willie Nelson, on the Legends Corner mural on the side of the honky-tonk bar near Music City's historic Ryman Auditorium.

"They got me busier
than a one-legged man
in a butt-kicking contest."

— *Dolly Parton*

"I've known her since she was a baby.
Her father's a friend of mine,
and when she was born, he said,
'You just have to be her godmother,'
and I said, 'I accept.'
We never did do a big ceremony,
but I'm so proud of her, love her
and she's just like one of my own."

— *Dolly, on becoming honorary godmother to Miley Cyrus*

24" DOLL

"That's one of those
proud moments
where when people
started saying,
'So you call her Aunt Dolly,
is that your real aunt?'
'Yes, she is!'"

— *Miley Cyrus, on her pride
at having Dolly
on the set of her TV show*
Hannah Montana

"Little kids just see me in the street
and just point, 'Aunt Dolly!'
or 'Hi, Aunt Dolly!'
— and it's just been so cute."

— *Dolly, on her reception
after her appearances*
on Hannah Montana

In 2006, Dolly was a Kennedy Center honoree
for her lifetime contributions to the arts
and was feted, along with fellow honorees
singer and songwriter William "Smokey" Robinson,
musical theater composer Andrew Lloyd Webber,
film director Steven Spielberg,
and conductor Zubin Mehta, at a Blue Room reception
hosted by then President George W. Bush and Laura Bush.

President Donald Trump offered her
the Medal of Freedom twice,
but Dolly turned it down
due to her husband's illness
and the dangers of traveling
throughout the COVID-19 pandemic.

In April of 2020, she gave $1 million
to Vanderbilt University Medical Center,
which helped develop a COVID-19 vaccine.
She didn't get the jab right away,
saying that even at 75 years old,
she didn't want to "jump the line."

Dolly strongly encouraged everyone
to get vaccinated against COVID-19 when eligible
and performed a song celebrating her vaccination,
set to the tune of "Jolene."
Lyrics included the lines,
"Vaccine, vaccine, vaccine, vaccine/
I'm begging of you please don't hesitate/
Vaccine, vaccine, vaccine, vaccine/'
Cos once you're dead, then that's a bit too late."

"I am honored and humbled by their intention
but I have asked the leaders of the state legislature
to remove the bill from any and all consideration.
Given all that's going on in the world,
I don't think putting me on a pedestal
is appropriate at this time."

— Dolly, via Twitter,
rejecting Tennessee lawmakers' bill
to erect a statue of her
at the Tennessee Capitol

"Find out who you are
and do it on purpose."

— *Dolly Parton*

"I do write a lot of children's songs,
and I'm going to do a children's television show,
which also means I'll be doing a lot of albums.
So I do hope my future will hold
a lot of things for children."

— *Dolly Parton*

"I think there are some stereotypes associated with the area, especially in rural Appalachia. I think it's great that we have a figure like Dolly Parton, who comes from the area and is able to shed light on it and be an ambassador."

— *Dr. Lynn Sacco, University of Tennessee associate professor, who teaches the course "Dolly's America"*

Dolly was awarded the Living Legend Medal
by the U.S. Library of Congress in 2004,
for her contributions to the cultural heritage of the United States.

"She's always writing books or writing songs
or doing something for people
or helping people in Tennessee totally."

— *Lily Tomlin, on Dolly's charitable spirit*

In response to the 2016 Great Smoky Mountains wildfires, Dolly, along with a number of other country music artists, participated in a telethon to raise money for victims of the fires.

Dolly has founded a number of charitable
and philanthropic organizations.
The chief among them is the Dollywood Foundation,
which manages a number of projects
to bring education and poverty relief
to East Tennessee, where she grew up.

"If your actions create a legacy
that inspires others to dream more,
learn more, do more and become more,
then, you are an excellent leader."

— *Dolly Parton*

"I started the Imagination Library over 20 years ago in honor of my father, who was never able to read or write. So my dad got to help me with it, and he felt very proud for me to be doing that and to involve him in it. He got to live long enough to see it doing well. He got a kick out of people calling me the book lady."

— *Dolly, on the 1995 launch of Imagination Library,*
which has distributed books to millions of children world-wide

"God didn't let me have kids
so everybody's kids could be mine."

— *Dolly Parton*

"I love story songs
because I've always loved books."

— *Dolly Parton*

Dolly has written seven books over the decades,
including two illustrated children's books
(*Coat of Many Colors* and *I Am a Rainbow*),
several memoirs (including *My Life and Other Unfinished Business*
and *Dolly Parton, Songteller: My Life in Lyrics*),
and even a cookbook, *Dolly's Dixie Fixin's: Love,
Laughter and Lots of Good Food.*

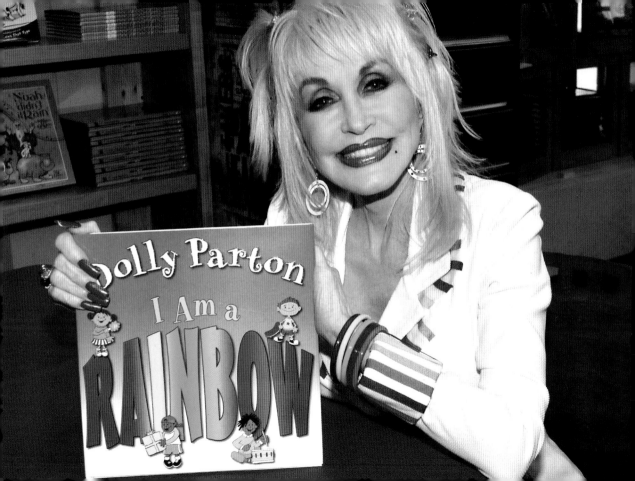

She is a co-owner of The Dollywood Company,
which operates the theme park Dollywood,
a dinner theater, Dolly Parton's Stampede,
the waterpark Dollywood's Splash Country,
and the Dream More Resort and Spa, all in Pigeon Forge.
Dollywood is the 24th-most-popular theme park
in the United States, with three million visitors per year.

"I don't like to get messed up.
I'm gonna have some handsome man mess it up,
I don't want some ride doing it."

— *Dolly, on never riding the rides at Dollywood*

In 2022, Dolly Parton's Dollywood Parks & Resorts
announced it would pay all tuition costs, fees,
and books for employees who pursue higher education.

"Whenever I see Dolly Parton
trending on social media,
I don't even have to look
to be pretty confident
it's for something positive.
Then I do look,
and it gets even better."

— *Author Dayton Ward, on Dolly, via Twitter*

"Dream more,
learn more,
care more,
and be more."

— *Dolly Parton*

"We need to carry that Christmas spirit
of peace on Earth, and loving one another.
We need to carry that into the new year. . .
We can't save the world,
but we can save the world
we're living in."

— *Dolly Parton*

"Don't get so busy making a living
that you forget to make a life."

— *Dolly Parton*

"I've struggled enough in my life
to be appreciated and understood.
I've had to go against all kinds of people
through the years just to be myself.
I think everybody should be allowed to be
who they are, and to love who they love.
I don't think we should be judgmental.
Lord, I've got enough problems of my own
to pass judgment on somebody else."

— *Dolly Parton*

"Stop this attitude
that older people ain't any good anymore!
We're as good as we ever were —
if we ever were any good."

– *Dolly Parton*

"I don't know what the big deal is about old age.
Old people who shine from the inside
look 10 to 20 years younger."

— *Dolly Parton*

"This year my birthday wish
is a call for kindness.
We can't just hope for a brighter day,
we have to work for a brighter day.
Love too often gets buried
in a world of hurt and fear.
So today, January 19th,
let's get to unearthing love."

— *Dolly, via Twitter, on her 75th birthday in 2021*

"I've been around a long time.
Long enough for people to realize
that there's more to me
than the big hair
and the phoney stuff."

— *Dolly Parton*

"I never have changed in my taste,
and the things that I love,
and the way that I act, and all that.
I never wanted to change,
I just wanted to be successful,
and be able to do more things
for more people,
and for myself as well."

— *Dolly Parton*

"I've always believed things would go well,
and I dreamed that they would
even before I was in high school.
I always wanted to be a star.
It just seemed natural to me.
I now know, of course,
that I've been very lucky."

— *Dolly Parton*

"I like to think I've been a good example
and an inspiration to some people.
And some people say that about me,
but I'm just going about my work
and doing what I do best.
I'm a very professional 'Me.'"

— *Dolly Parton*

In 2021, she was included on the Time 100,
Time magazine's annual list of
the 100 most influential people in the world.

"Life is something we buy a ticket to every day
—and it doesn't come with popcorn."

— *Dolly Parton*

"Above everything else I've done,
I've always said I've had more guts
than I've got talent."

— *Dolly Parton*

"... I never got discouraged or disheartened—
I knew it would be there.
I felt I could out step anything that came in my way.
I really think that's why I've been successful because
I have so much determination
and believed so strongly that
everything would turn out good."

— *Dolly Parton*

"I'm never going to retire.
I just want to do greater work.
As mom would say,
I'm letting the spirit lead me."

— *Dolly Parton*

"I hope to die right in the middle of a song
and right on the stage doing what I love to do.
I hope to be about 120 when that happens."

— *Dolly Parton*

"Life is a song to me."

— *Dolly Parton*

PHOTOGRAPHY CREDITS

ABBREVIATIONS
ASP = Alamy Stock Photo
SS = Shutterstock.com
DT = Dreamstime.com
LOC = Library of Congress

Front cover: AFF | Alamy Stock Photo
Back cover: Sheri Lynn Behr | Alamy Stock Photo
Butterfly background: Embe2006 | Dreamstime.com

2–3 Sahroe/SS; 4 PictureLux|The Hollywood Archive/ASP; 8 Album/ASP; 11 sandy young/ASP; 12 Pictorial Press/ASP; 15 Ronald Grant Archive /ASP; 17 Keystone Press/ASP; 18 Media Punch/ASP; 21 CelebrityArchaeology.com/ASP; 22 LOC; 25 Records/ASP; 26 Media Punch/ASP; 29 Pictorial Press/ASP; 31 CSU Archives|Everett Collection/ASP; 32 Pictorial Press/ASP; 35 Media Punch/ASP; 36 Album/ASP; 39 Pictorial Press/ASP; 41 LOC; 42 Curtis Hilbun/ASP; 45 Tammie Arroyo/ASP; 47 Media Punch/ASP; 49 Everett Collection Inc/ASP; 50 Pictorial Press/ASP; 52 TCD/Prod.DB/ASP; 55 Pictorial Press/ASP; 56 CSU Archives|Everett Collection/ASP; 59 Curtis Hilbun|AFF-USA/ASP; 60 Pictorial Press/ASP; 63 Moeller Talent Inc. Nashville; 64 Pictorial Press/ASP; 67 Pictorial Press/ASP; 69 Brett Jordan/Creative Commons Attribution 2.0 Generic; 70 Tammie Arroyo/ASP; 72 PictureLux|The Hollywood Archive/ ASP; 75 Sandollar Productions|Album/ASP; 76 PictureLux|The Hollywood Archive/ASP; 79 LOC; 80 Curtis Hilbun/ASP; 82 LOC; 85 Pictorial Press/ASP; 86 Abaca Press/ASP; 89 PictureLux|The Hollywood Archive/ASP; 90 Pictorial Press/ ASP; 93 Curtis Hilbun/ASP; 94 Pictorial Press/ASP; 96 Tor Erik Schrꬨder/ASP; 99 TCD/Prod.DB/ASP; 100 Terence Faircloth/ Creative Commons license Attribution-NonCommercial-NoDerivs 2.0 Generic; 102 Pictorial Press/ASP; 105 Everett Collection Inc/ASP; 106 Pictorial Press/ASP; 109 Tammie Arroyo/ASP; 110 Kathy Hutchins/SS; 113 Curtis Hilbun/ASP; 114 Curtis Hilburn/ASP; 117 Tammie Arroyo/ASP; 118 Bart Sherkow/ SS; 120 Curtis Hilbun/ASP; 123 Yui Mok/ASP; 124 Archive PL/ ASP; 126 Sandollar Productions|Album/ASP; 129 Media Punch/ ASP; 130 Barry King/ASP; 133 The Hollywood Archive/ASP; 134 Pictorial Press/ASP; 136 Blueee/ASP; 138 Adam Scull/ASP; 141 ZUMA Press/ASP; 142 MIKE BLAKE/ASP; 145 PictureLux|The Hollywood Archive/ASP; 147 PictureLux|The Hollywood Archive/ASP; 148 Jim Ruymen/ASP; 150 Media Punch/ASP; 153 Curtis Hilbun/ASP; 154 Sbukley /DT; 156 Kathy Hutchins/SS; 158 Matteo Omied/ASP; 161 Harry Langdon|Rock Negatives|Media Punch/ASP; 162 Collection Christophel/ASP; 164 PictureLux|The Hollywood Archive/ASP; 167 Media Punch/ASP; 168 Daniel Dempster Photography/ASP; 171 Pictorial Press/ASP; 172 Pictorial Press/ASP; 175 PictureLux|The Hollywood Archive/ ASP; 176 Pictorial Press/ASP; 179 Pictorial Press/ASP; 180 Media Punch/ASP; 183 Curtis Hilbun/ASP; 184 Media Punch/ASP; 187 Concert Photos/ASP; 189 Curtis Hilbun/ASP; 190 Abaca Press/ASP; 193 Tammie Arroyo/ASP; 194 Media Punch/ASP;